MAN ON A
MISSION MEMOIRS

MAN ON A MISSION MEMOIRS

DARRYL MINCEY

authorHOUSE®

AuthorHouse™ LLC
1663 Liberty Drive
Bloomington, IN 47403
www.authorhouse.com
Phone: 1-800-839-8640

Published by AuthorHouse 09/03/2014

ISBN: 978-1-4969-3840-4 (sc)
ISBN: 978-1-4969-3839-8 (e)

ABOUT THE BOOK

For People Who Need A Miracle or Desire To Experience The Power Of God.

DEDICATION

This is dedicated to word of life covenant church.

CONTENTS

THE WAKE UP CALL

We are praying to be used by God for being obedient and we are in the light of God in Ephesians 5 verse 13 it's the wake up call every morning and God will tell you to wake up and a whole of nourishment for the spirit and to rise up to stir us and now were responsible for it because of the ways to accomplish to desire and face it because the people need steering and a Godly motivation and pass the arise from the dead and make a provision to be in the light and to be moving and the whole thing will be whole and God will wake us up from it and how are you desperate are you for God? Well the answer is it's a wonderful experience and to know him to help our financial needs and to have to touch God. Do we have a mind to share with the Lord and go with him because it is the spirit of living and a whole existence of the giving indifferent things how to be cool.

And your heart to redeem the time the days are bad in Luke 8 verse 40 says the detail and come to pass and in people's hearts and the details in the story and when you preach in the bible and you in the word and he is never late and kind of participation of a push because of a desperate situation of the focus on deck and it means to be fasten to set on fire and therefore and people to desire to make it right and make it comfort and in peace and it will become a miracle and be in a crowd and do anything to be one of them and be in the flow and the bible says to work with people and with love with many of times to share with others even to wittiness to focus a pattern to work and the Holy Ghost wants to come in the meetings of the church and the door will be open all the time and the spirit will rise up and the setting of the people will wake up the spirit and the feeding power of the Holy Spirit and read the book.

Faith is a understanding right out the old and put into the new and bring the ark of God and will not struggle and means to excess of the work that God did for us and in 1st Kings chapter 3 verse 5 says David's heart was right but the behavior was wrong and in verse 9 is to produce a rightly judge of the root and gift will be given to cause the honor of light and the word of Solomon excess of knowledge of the right reason to love the Lord in the heart of their heart and explore the wisdom in Proverbs chapter 9 says wisdom has built the house of wisdom and achieve it and raise up a generation (Matt 7 verse 24) hearing and doing to build a rock of experience of the right foundation of the house and the presence of God it is the anointing of truth will set you free.

Darryl L. Mincey Man on a Mission Inc.

July 18, 1997

TOTAL ADJUSTING ON FAITH

Major adjustment of the word of God the ultimate is the cross and sometimes is the greater ability is the obedient being in the Lord Jesus and the will of God and when you find the will of God to do others and maybe to adjust and never allow to follow a decision to make and furthermore what adjustments what you make a measure of that foundation of 30 to 100 fold and what you given to need to adjust to have a relation is the holy spirit and the step of obedience and to be available to him and have a purpose to serve and a season of the adjusting of the word knowing what to bring a great foundation of the spirit and to finish a pattern of peace and to create a purpose of his kingdom and a total dependence on God, faith and his wisdom and his great knowledge and we can come upon to plant to see and touch and listen and have the experience the balance of the word and to the devotion of the spirit and the divine the disciple and when you lift you up and to believe in it.

Do not fear with situation during the knowledge of strength of faith and the fruit of the spirit and the fruit of faith and one thing looking towards the balance of peace.

JUSTIFIED BY FAITH

Understanding justifying your faith it is like a tool of everything what you need in encouragement of the holy spirit and let God's voice show you the key of rightenous and to renewing of your mind and to make sure the kite will fly and to swing loose like an angel of faith and God will go through that and the pleasing the rhema and led to the sons and daughters of

God and the outcome to bless people to begin to start a 30 to 100 fold in the spirit and a strong feeling to have a 100 fold in your Christian life and having a piece of mind and the peace of focus and a powerful force and the nations of the Lord will teach us to the teaching of the Lord and your calling will be a prayer information and the skill of listening is very important and be able to focus of God and being led to the spirit is not easy to obtain but we need the will of God and one thing your mind will be transformed and never lose that transformation by renewing of your mind and the days to rebuild in the spirit and established the foundation in the house of God and the anointing is very important to us.

Darryl L. Mincey Man on a Mission Inc.

8-22-97

THE COMMISSION

The commission is a release because to teach us to have a value to commit what we know and what we think and to plant a seed and to choose the word of life and to teach and preach the word and cast a vision and to have wisdom in the Book of Proverbs says that we must have wisdom in our hearts and never be feared in this because it is the refreshing of impartation of the rhythm and to restore the impact of the church and the people must walk towards the lord and to explore the reasons of being a Christian and taught all over the world and release the attitudes in the foundation of the real thing and to except a special Christian and to walk of healing and the message is great and in 1st Corinthians chapter 13 {The healing source of praying and to accept what we need and to have a tool of the identification of healing and the thrill of victory and the agony of defeat and we will never be defeated in one split second and the gift from God will never failed and the ministry is a high call on Jesus and to prepare of compassion.

And more will excite you because it is God and the exportation and the great experience in the book of acts says the acts of healing and feeling and there is 5 principles is the principal of faith, the principal of sin, the principal of life, compassion of anointing and the principal of understanding and to know why we need it and if you have a bad hair day the wall of faith will come up with a plan to discover the gift and to work on it a be a witness for God and use it like a tool of healing and to feel the power of faith and to create the the miracles and the area of sin will be removed and the power of faith will rise up and be victorious and the anointing of God's work.

Darryl L. Mincey Man on a Mission Inc.

8-21-97

A TEAM'S PURPOSE

The book of proverbs says to keep hold on the instruction do not let go and to act on God's direction in a daily devotions and to keep a straight path and he will fill all your ways to be sure and the beginning of wisdom is this to get wisdom and whatever else you get is to get an insight and to follow the unity of the holy spirit and in 1st Corinthians 9 verse 24 says to exercise self control and one thing is 3 things is the purpose is one your race to win and to run straight to the goal and don't get tired of doing right and do not get discouraged and to give up and to be kind to everyone and to pray all the time.

The plan is to discipline your body and train to use all the pieces of God's armour provided for you and the prize is standing safe against all the strategies and the tricks of the enemy and the heavenly reward that never disappears and we will live with Christ and we will sit and rule with him and always remain faithful to us and always carries out his promises and this team will have a goal and win the victory.

Darryl L. Mincey Man on a Mission Inc.

8-21-97

RESPONSE BY FAITH

Without faith it will be impossible to operate and it is impossible to work with God and please and it's not desire to it but must reveal it and make it happen and known when people come to reveal it.

And impact towards Christ and when God speaks to you it's great because you will be resent to response not to resent or a principale or concept and a bad person and you will have faith and you will respond to God that is radical.

It is impossible to read it and require by faith but you must do it when he says it or always know what God can do and we must obey God can see and does it when you have a word from God you can be obedient and faith has a response to a person and to be assign to it and don't look at the circumstances and decide what he can do and let God speak to you even your financial situation.

Even the crisis of belief is what God speaks to and the it will come and will help you in that situation and be arrange even when you have a situation you must trust God and accomplish it and provide including to refresh your mind in the spirit and have the boldness of refreshing in a situation to forgive and forget but sometimes it is very hard sometimes even when you plant a seed that does not grow it needs water to refresh and to be filles by the Holy ghost.

And also telling the truth to others the refreshing point to stretch to believe and assemble to shake together to counsel one person to another and realize of healing of anointing will come and faith and togetherness and love will unite.

Faith is in the heart and the fource of faith will come to you in every thought because the head must obey in Jesus and see it and see the spirit and light it up storing a data and the foundation of the root will grow even the children must be discipline to their parents and the flow in that appetite of the areas will scan the focus of the spirit and keep the candlestick shine and bright.

During the words of knowledge we must obey and practice what you preach and try to prophet the word of God and bless them in the spiritual realm even the words will be anointing also.

Darryl L. Mincey Man on a mission Inc.

THE PROTECTION FOR THE HOUSE

Pray for the hedge and your faithfulness in God and give intentally to perform and be willing and never be approach without the offering and represent the talent and multiply and build a protection to our house.

Burnt stone of the heat of battle but they are easily shock not to handle but the soldiers don't know what's gonna happen and some of them maybe they are useless and God cannot use the stones because they can't provide the foundation of it because burnt stones cannot be replace of the building projects and the prophets of the foundation of the organization of the vision but God will give you the love of Christ and the church build it up but the foxes will mess it up the building but the spirit will knock off the fox either way a little fox will mess you up and unbalance it Neh. chapter 1 verse 1.

Along with the ancestor and need more prople and more radical worshiping and pour out and soak it in and deliverance and a lifestyle and the bitterness will be knock off and rather be crazy and struggle with it and church is a place of love and God is very important to us and we need that feeling and to keep that motion and don't mess up even the division because the enemy will fight you in the properganda and the negative things and the bitter things and poverty will go through but in prayer it will not come.

And see a pattern that the moment when God touches you and re program you its like a song playing over and over again and like a rehersial inside you and the Lord's will watch over the ministry and the ministry of hearing the healing inward and to connect and fornication and the expert of healing and set the people free and must talk to the unsaved and to be save and to start from square one is to deal with the enemy and knock him down and a circle of influence {Neh chapter 4 verse 15 to 21} defense and offence and comes a period of times of a strong city and the church is the defense and obvious of it when the armour had a key of victory and build a place for the poor and he will defend it.

But the gasp are open the enemies will come in but if the gasp are all seal they will be protected by the Holy spirit and it will be fortified and it will focus the foundation and will be able including the Godly thoughts of love joy and peace and the spirit of your mind and something of the stimulus reaction and the rival of the Holy Spirit will be there but when it comes in that will be a response and you are not seeing it the hooks are there but when you are saved the hooks will be release and the spirit of might will set you free and a fast building will be complete.

TRY TO SAVED UNSAVED SOULS

Do not try to approach them they will approach you and to try to have a rapture the revelation and the normal way of life and to minster the unsaved because if they don't Jesus and try to establish your goals or theirs the victory will not stand the activity what people do need and sharing the good news and have a expert to defeat the enemy and to cast out demons and set the unsaved people free and the 20% you need and to know right now the 80% of salvation by this and be successful and to revive and to share the gospel and understand the respond of it.

And to have a pattern to respond is to have the great credit to illustrate and to train to do it and to provide what it is and the study of understanding of the testimony is very important until you do something of any skill and try to do it and the first time they don't do it in that matter they will need practice to be confident and to have a victory and be better in the spirit and to have miracles even the gift of a testimony.

Darryl L. Mincey Man on a Mission Inc.

August 27, 1997

FAITHFUL TO SERVE GOD

How to serve him is to recognize your spiritual life and attend your ministry and suddenly not to hold back because God needs your prayers and wants us to present an answer to it and have the strings and in Isaiah chapter 51 says the woman was not prepare because she was in trouble in judgement and the bible is not a boring book it is a tool and have a balance it is a balance to help you be fulfilled and be obedient and a close thing to God and the destiny and Jacob never had a motive of a winning situation and a covenant of Jacob's fulfilling personal history and the prayer closet and to perform and to plant your life in the power of life and also the kingdom of life and to be courage and the book of Genesis chapter 11 is to stay in the rival and do not desire in that direction and fulfilled his pattern and proceed in that purpose for life and a lot of energy and never have a baggage {Acts 7 verse 1 and 2 the father is a God of glory and have the appearance and have faith.} and in Galatians 3 verse 8 all the angels are representatives in Heaven and to unite and have a giant of them and physically no way to interfere and never obtain in Deu chapter 29 verses 1 & 2 says that God is well able and in Deut chapter 3 it is a good point of measuring the feeling and sensing a giant of greatness of the measurement of God and in Gensus chapter six says the angel were dressed in white and there work is peaceful and to treat other people good not bad they were like giants and were great.

THE ENCOURAGEMENT OF FAITH

Through our times we must be obedient with the father because we must stay alert and also in prayer and the most of the times we must proceed and the door will be open always and preaching the word will always be strong and to be courage to one to another and to get involved in our ministry and do it out of love for Christ and to others to help new Christians become strong even to influence others for the gospel and give the good news about faith and love and the statis of it.

But we should not to be fear because the ruler of lies or tempter can affect the spiritual world but Jesus defeated the enemies when he died on the cross for our sins and Jesus rose up again to bring us new life at the proper time and God will throw the enemies out for ever and the great joy for Christians come out of the and into the new because they must be fruitful and to grow in faith and to share with other Christians even to direct them to honestly and everything has a purpose of the the right moment and to support to others.

A pattern to learn and equip to obtain 3 things in your faithful spiritual life is to rejoice, keep praying, and to give thanks it will go easier and to be joyful for the faith they need to grow and grow in the spirit. Furthermore the blessing of faith will provide what the people need to gain a level and to believe a blessing for the high calling of greatness and the movement of faith will be the truth of it according to the bible and to create the faith and movement of truth to one to another and give us the light to shine and to measure it because it needs to mature by the word of faith and the condition of freedom and remain in a peaceful situation and to plant the fruit of encouragement of strength and you will be blessed and victorious by the Holy Spirit and never be self-destructed and never be empty in your spiritual system even your strength and giving how to do the right thing and your spiritual growth and learn how to trust Jesus and to relate an encouragement of God -Centered faith and the target of spiritual direction of a distance of knowing what we see in the harvest and the kingdom of God and be victorious in your Christian love walk and the walk of faith.

Purify the encouragement of faith and love by the word and the goal of victory and we must develop one by one obeying the word and the scriptures and the anointing of the new birth of Christians and develop character and direction of praying in your personal giving and your spiritual growth and we must ???

THE ALTAR OF TRUTH

The church world is picking up the pieces and find the truth and to result to find the pieces and also many things in the spirit world and find out a pattern to fix things because what we know about the receiving of the church and the experience of God - Centered people and to build a divine arrangement for the subject of the emerging priesthood and the anointing in Exodus chapter 30 and in Matthew 27 there is a new priesthood and we must live in today and in verse 45 we must have the privage and in our heart and to divine the vail and the worship must come in our heart and the ultermine in our heart and the altar in our sense and the rewinding of our spirit and God is meeting a specification of arrange the dwelling place and God will meet you all day long and the breakthrough and have that believe and what you do and your dead body and God will give you a re-lived body and a life and a century to develop the altar and what we do for us it is the building for altars and the pastors become a priest and the the basic of the meeting from God and we will come in covant and in a living way and to fill the glory of greatness and the glory will come in our house and each other and much more and a full contact and a new life with a thought from God and the development of the true one and the book of divine nature.

In Exodus chapter 20 the present will change you by wainting for the image of great things and the adjustment of the voice of God and a personal relationship of the lord and we must plant that plan and the issues and the deliverance and what you say about those things of their hearts of great changes of rejoying presence of their require next of the meaefist of the growing and hear the word and the future and to simply hear his voice and hear the commandments and to hear the plan the purpose in the book of exodus chapter chapter 30 and the priest of the high calling of God and to look for some people to find the great thing of their lives and the pressure will be remove and in Hebrews chapter 8 the anointing of freedom and to bring truth and to arouse what you gain in the future and in verse 10 of Exodus we cannot pedal backward we must pedal forward and a privage and not to icons and to give you great experts and to occur to breathe on life and one thing the sin must get out.

In our altars in our place of burning incense to coming and to God and make a place that which enters the Holy place and to motivication when people's hearts are harden on hurt and that strange things but God will use the fragrance and will use to glorified the progress and the offer that strange fire and a abuse the struggling form and the relationship with a twisted version of our younger lives and we offer something and shall not offer the situation and void the tradition and God wants clear deck and advise it and to forecast the altars even the call of truth and the form of God and to walk of them and to summit them and willing to obtain the wrong thing to get in a jam and reckoning the old turf and let the new turf and to measure it and the hooks will come out and you will healed and this change is radical and serving God.

Giving a deal to clean up the mess and have the opportunity in Philippians 2 says it time to clean up the deck and this is the beloved one and clear the present and pleased the great relationship by this by this one and the present things right now is the place of the right and to preach it and do the right thing in the kingdom of God and the anointing by God and re-unite them and step with a bound to seek the face of God and just attend and to accomplished the feelings of worship and what we can offer and looking for it and lift them up to the voice of God and to believe the book of 2nd Chronicles verse 12 bring glorified and to multiply and the presence of it is very important to clear the deck.

In the book of Acts Jesus is the standard one for us because he was made manifest to destroy the enemies and God will give you the testimony to have a believer's commission in Acts chapter 8 verse 4 says that we are no bad force to take the believers out of their home in Jerusalem and with them with the gospel and in Mark chapter 10 verse 29 and you in God's faith in the anointing and raise up the standard one and the high calling and to prepare for this and the habits of worship in Jesus and to manifest the feeling of the spirit and to be changed by the spirit and the prayers and the word of wisdom and the working of miracles and to cover these things and glorified by it and to contend and confirm the word of transformation and to make up the difference and touch the head of the garment and the angel of the lord will be there and the spirit of truth will be there and to remove the junk of our minds and love in our hearts and to touch others and to talk to them and it will changed us and nothing will stand in our way and whatever it takes and praying of God and the presence of glory will be there to set people free and have a breakthrough and to embrace not religion but Jesus and to maintain a present form.

We must stay with God and his kingdom because it is a investment to that standard procedure and comes right out of that old and bring in the new and never bring out the religion with us and never have a challenge to think about it and be willing to go there and get more from God and the importance of the book of Joshua says the main thing is the information and the greatest purpose to teach to one another to obey the Holy Spirit and the purpose is there anyway and never be denied and clearing what we know and break the explosion and to see the moment of the great anointing of the oil.

And the things of the divine point of vieu and the real thing abd the real thing and God will do wonders for you and the thing around us will be a blessed one and do it right and give you that altar of light of life and the covenant and the movement and God's power to bring it to you and watch the movement and the people will fear out of trouble and the fear of man of the mist of Jordan and cover the whole rock of the river Jordan and the vessel of God and need to break off the stuff and he does not sit back and attend to go forward and gives us a new realm and a different one and to achieve things and come to pass and stand still and God will do the work and the breath of God will breathe upon it and see what we talk about it and the presence of God will be with you and to visit the church and the season of the seasons and the moment of the city will be lit up and the anointing of the harvest will bring a sweet thing of the bible and to move and occupy a greater purpose and a world wide change and to teach the people of the issues of Jesus and the situation of tomorrow and sanctify what we do for the heart.

To cover a revelation and to cover a anointing to set free is to feed the word and to operate the glory of God and the priesthood will be filled by the Holy Spirit and everyone will be filled with joy and understanding and having the word of God will fill our hearts with greatness and reliable to use the instruments of God and he will fix it up and the touch of God will be there and everyone will be anointed and will be bless by it and in the book of Exodus chapter 30 says a special mixture of the oil of the inside and the wound inside you will be healed and the oil of joy inside you will be good also and to pour out the spirit and to communicate in the kingdom of heaven of the greatness and contact.

In Acts 13 verse 2 the fellowship for us in a hence for fellowship and give us a victory in Christ and seeking in the Holy Spirit and have a great miracle in the kingdom of Christ and appling the account of this is very important and the blessing the word and prosper and stick it in your spirit and to the 60 to 100 fold and God had a better covenant and a better demonstration and with the lord our strength and the lifestyle in the spirit and transfigure the bound of glory and to reveal to obey and to listen and will be signs and wonders and the holy place for the lord turning to a sight of obedience and hearing the word.

I am the anointed one and Christ lives inside me and a proper way to be glorified and in 2nd Kings the 2nd chapter says how to believe the new anointing and have a double portion and a new wave of explosion of a brand new anointing of magnification and to receive it and show the ways of different things of the spirit of God one is to stay in the spirit, 2 to stick with it, 3 the focus the anointing, 4 is to have knowledge, and 5 is to minister to them and thats why we throw the bad things out and bring in the new and have a power to impact and have a internal life and change the atmosphere and to grow to a mature thing to the lord and to anoint them to reveal and a divine relationship and to sense it and have the vision and be in the will of God and set the prophetic emotion and wherever who has the word they will received the following and God will take the nation by form and in 2nd Kings 2 verse 8 says the way to show what we need to have a ministry and to reveal to preach the word and let God speak in your heart and to preach the gospel and the last thing is this the body of Christ and to be in harmony in the spirit and to flow and flow and if God did not ordained us he would not love us in the spirit but he does and we must show the world and in 2 Chronicles the 13th chapter in verse 2 the inner cities must come together and also the suburbs and to combined and to be equalized and tear down the walls of racium and see the move of God and fill it.

Focus but never accused but never condemned and go and sin no more you throw away the life styles the word is total forgiveness in Luke chapter 7 the holy ghost power when we feel the anointing power and to affecting to this power inside people desires in verse 36 the change the flavor and which he does- to whom is forgiven you is right now is clean and a peaceful way and the giving of faith and God wants you there Psalms 139.

Darryl L. Mincey Man on a Mission Inc

September 14, 1997

FEEDING THE BREATH OF LIFE

Most of us must be fed on the spirit and to minister the people and to plant certain fruits of revelation and gather the express the high calling and to mandate and done proper and to divine the water of life and the time to prepare and free to obey is a chapter of a gift and make it clearer and make it happen and also the breakthrough in the spirit of life and what we do and to invite the people into God's heaven and to teach us because we do not believe in the word religion because it is a bad word it not safe and burn the midnight oil and never read the scripture but you will still be lifted up in the spirit and have a fine knowledge and the great works in the earth and in the book of Corinthians says to follow the pastor and led by the son of God and there is 3 things in this is one being led, 2 obey the word, and 3 is to require and to relate and the experience the gift and what you led in the spirit and God will give you different things and gave them to the ghuuch and to read the bible also because the condition of prophecy is very important and must have a condition part and the most of the churches and the Holy Ghost and the working of miracles and the dose of the injection and blinds out the anger and hear more of God and do not be a gangster of anger but a lifetime member of the Lord and learn the gift of the Spirit and the remembrance of the church and to obey the holy one and the rule of worship of glory and the great fruit of the spirit and to attend great things and the breakthrough will be there and the positioning of giving and having faith is very important the find the seed of the harvest and planting the right one is good and to the gold hearted.

And if we was not around Jesus we can be into big trouble all around and we will be written off and get down but we are not down in Jesus land and have the power of influence and ghanged one life and one word to one person and to millions in time and one of the thing is having stock at word of life and invest and get something that is bow of ministry and the arrows that you have to identify a small type of boundaries but your garden of Eden was Adam's stopping ground and he made the mistakes and thats why he learn in the society and to go in that salvation and a prophetic word in every church and into your life and a perfect time and sense the phrase of the word and this is which is spoken and meet you and to have a destiny in your life and to develop and the household of the church and which of that which is spoken.

And also have a certain road of the division of walking the right road and comes in the spirit and seek the Lord and all things will happen and to take a bow of ministry and practice the anointing and aim the substance of the direction of the word of churches and to be surrounded by the laying on the hands (1st Tim 1 verse 18) fight off the good fight and stand before God and drawn to him (still hold on and hold it) working that line of division and have a breakthrough to God and God does color inside the line and when you have the bow and arrow and the weapons of war and to direct and give to the enemies nothing because we are a cooperate church and to fight your ministry and have that gift when you have called for it in the occupation of ministry you hold it and to be large and to stand in the place of high calling and in a month it will be large and it will occupy a smooth and what we know about the aim and to direct them even the window of opportunity and creation will develop a straight narrow and have a influence and the training the opening present and when it opens you take your best shot and the fire the source of gross not the net to pull you down from the sunshine to the heart of the expectation of gross and the Holy Spirit and the deliverance from sin and aim that ministry to go forward and to be amazed and God's people to be free from guilt and the content to strike the enemy and knock him down and prefer to that and all the word you have use it and to live on the that and live on the impact and to unfold and to respond and to unite and to between the future of the impact of authority to be called on God and to be stronger and in 1st Samuel 13 says the windows of ministry the spear and use of it and the most of it your ministry and will go stronger and stronger to the Lord.

To feed the environment to be fed of the Spirit to have a vieu for the body of Christ and to connect the value to know the truth and to practice what you preach and to believe in a message and the idea of great trust and never have a short notice of a missing link of that situation because its like a oil and never dig a well and to be one accord and a generation and some place of time will be introduce in a rival in a strange thing in your life and to be set free in the Holy Spirit and the experience of the test of a favor and to be tracted and you have a relationship in Jesus and begin to move and to reform and never missed the window of opportunity of a shield of protection to design to come in that matter and never be in a situation to be smash up because you will be and going to a level for a high calling in Ephesians Chapter 2 verse 1 and to receive the knowledge of Christ and the cooperation of a window of destiny and wisdom and revelation of the destiny and to the in spiritual growth in the Lord and to magnify the connection to grow in the future and to attend to preach the feeders and have a strong perfection and never have a combustion to our ministry and affect the enemy so he will not mess you up in that form.

These things we studied to plug in the future and the kingdom of God is the anointing of the spirit and make it click and the feeding by the word and to cast out demons and devour them and to commit in your ministry and to retain and great commission to be set free and the opportunities to get the people on track and the basis the discipline and to connect the missing piece of God's work

Darryl L. Mincey Man on a Mission Inc.

September 21, 1997

THE ALTAR OF TRUTH

The church world is picking up the pieces and find the truth and to result to find the pieces and also many things in the spirit world and find out a pattern to fix things because what we know about the receiving of the church and the experience of God - Centered people and to build a divine arrangement for the subject of the emerging priesthood and the anointing in Exodus chapter 30 and in Matthew 27 there is a new priesthood and we must live in today and in verse 45 we must have the privage and in our heart and to divine the vail and the worship must come in our heart and the ultermine in our heart and the altar in our sense and the re winding of our spirit and God is meeting a specification of arrange the dwelling place and God will meet you all day long and the breakthrough and have that believe and what you do and your dead body and God will give you a re-lived body and a life and a century to develop the altar and what we do for us it is the building for altars and the pastors become a priest and the the basic of the meeting from God and we will come in covant and in a living way and to fill the glory of greatness and the glory will come in our house and each other and much more and a full contact and a new life with a thought from God and the development of the true one and the book of divine nature.

In Exodus chapter 20 the present will change you by wainting for the image of great things and the adjustment of the voice of God and a personal relationship of the lord and we must plant that plan and the issues and the deliverance and what you say about those things of their hearts of great changes of rejoying presence of their require next of the meaefist of the growing and hear the word and the future and to simply hear his voice and hear the commandments and to hear the plan the purpose in the book of exodus chapter chapter 30 and the priest of the high calling of God and to look for some people to find the great thing of their lives and the pressure will be remove and in Hebrews chapter 8 the anointing of freedom and to bring truth and to arouse what you gain in the future and in verse 10 of Exodus we cannot pedal backward we must pedal forward and a privage and not to icons and to give you great experts and to occur to breathe on life and one thing the sin must get out.

In our altars in our place of burning incense to coming and to God and make a place that which enters the Holy place and to motivication when people's hearts are harden on hurt and that strange things but God will use the fragrance and will use to glorified the progress and the offer that strange fire and a abuse the struggling form and the relationship with a twisted version of our younger lives and we offer something and shall not offer the situation and void the tradition and God wants clear deck and advise it and to forecast the altars even the call of truth and the form of God and to walk of them and to summit them and willing to obtain the wrong thing to get in a jam and reckoning the old turf and let the new turf and to measure it and the hooks will come out and you will healed and this change is radical and serving God.

Giving a deal to clean up the mess and have the opportunity in Philippians 2 says it time to clean up the deck and this is the beloved one abdclear the present and pleased the great relationship by this by this one and the present things right now is the place of the right and to preach it and do the right thing in the kingdom of God and the anointing by God and re-unite them and step with a bound to seek the face of God and just attend and to accomplished the feelings of worship and what we can offer and looking for it and lift them up to the voice of God and to believe the book of 2nd Chronicles verse 12 bring glorified and to multiply and the presence of it is very important to clear the deck.

JESUS THE STANDARD ONE:

Jesus made manifest to destroy the enemy and God will give you a testimony to have a believers commission in Acts chapter 8 verse 4 we do not have a force the believers out of their home in Jerusalem and with them with the gospel. In Mark 10 verse 29 and if you have God's faith in the anointing and raise up the standard and the high calling and to prepare the habits of worship in Jesus the manifest one of all and the prayers will have a world of vision and working of miracles and to cover these things and to be glorified by it attend and to confirm the word and the transformation and make up the difference and touch the head of the garment and the angel of God will be there and the spirit of truth and to attend what we know and to remove the debis and the angel will touch our hearts and to touch others and talk to them and the things of the church become Jesus and the authority of the organization will change us and and the praying will help us and the presence and the wings of God will set his people free and the breakthrough will embrace not religion but Jesus.

In Joshua Chapter 3 says to go with God and do something right and the form of the pasture will be willing to go in the kingdom of God and that is important for Joshua sats we have to be manifest the greatest things what we are and to teach others in the holy spirit and the purpose is there anyway and will never fail in that situation and the anointing of the oil.

And things of the divine the real thing and God will do wonders for you and things around and to be bless and do the right thing for Jesus and the light of the altar will bring the light of life and the covenant will bring the power and watch the moment and never be feared by it and the mist of the river Jordan and covering the whole rock and to break the stuff and the Lord does not want to sit you back he wants you to go forward and a new realm and to achieve to pass upon the breath of God and to breathe upon it and the presence of God will be there season after season and the moment of the city and to light the city also and bring up the harvest of toming and the sweet thing to know of a greater purpose of a world wide change to teach others and the issues of Jesus and the mist of the situation and what we do for the heart and Jesus will cover a revelation and to cover the anointing to set us free and to be fed and to be glorified by God and to be filled with the word of God will fix it up also with a great anointing and to bless it with a great mixture of the oil and a great healing of the purpose by it and the sound of the Holy Spirit will be a great connection to be wonderful.

Darryl L. Mincey Man on a Mission Inc.

September 24th 1997

FEEDING THE BREATH OF LIFE

Most of us must be fed on the spirit and to minister the people and to plant certain fruits of revelation and gather the express the high calling and to mandate and done proper and to divine the water of life and the time to prepare and free to obey is a chapter of a gift and make it clearer and make it happen and also the breakthrough in the spirit of life and what we do and to invite the people into God's heaven and to teach us because we do not believe in the word religion because it is a bad word it not safe and burn the midnight oil and never read the scripture but you will still be lifted up in the spirit and have a ine knowledge and the great works in the earth and in the book of Corinthians says to follow the pastor and led by the son of God and there is 3 things in this is one being led, 2 obey the word, and 3 is to require and to relate and the experience the gift and what you led in the spirit and God will give you different things and gave them to the ghuuch and to read the bible also because the condition of prophecy is very important and must have a condition part and the most of the churches and the Holy Ghost and the working of miracles and the dose of the injection and blinds out the anger and hear more of God and do not be a gangster of anger but a lifetime member of the Lord and learn the gift of the Spirit and the rememberance of the church and to obey the holy one and the rule of worship of glory and the great fruit of the spirit and to attend great things and the breakthrough will be there and the positioning of giving and having faith is very important the find the seed of the harvest and planting the right one is good and to the gold hearted.

And if we was not around Jesus we can be into big trouble all around and we will be written off and get down but we are not down in Jesus land and have the power of influence and ghanged one life and one word to one person and to millions in time and one of the thing is having stock at word of life and invest and get something that is bow of ministry and the arrows that you have to identify a small type of boundaries but your garden of Eden was Adam's stopping ground and he made the mistakes and thats why he learn in the society and to go in that salvation and a prophetic word in every church and into your life and a perfect time and sense the phrase of the word and this is which is spoken and meet you and to have a destiny in your life and to develop and the household of the church and which of that which is spoken.

And also have a certain road of the division of walking the right road and comes in the spirit and seek the Lord and all things will happen and to take a bow of ministry and practice the anointing and aim the substance of the direction of the word of churches and to be surrounded by the laying on the hands (1st Tim 1 verse 18) fight off the good fight and stand before God and drawn to him (still hold on and hold it) working that line of division and have a breakthrough to God and God does color inside the line and when you have the bow and arrow and the weapons of war and to direct and give to the enemy nothing because we are a cooperate church and to fight your ministry and have that gift when you have called for it in the occupation of ministry you hold it and to be large and to stand in the place of high calling and in a month it will be large and it will occupy a smooth and what we know about the aim and to direct them even the window of opportunity and creation will develop a straight narrow and have a influence and the training the opening present and when it opens you take your best shot and the fire the source of gross not the net to pull you down from the sunshine to the heart of the expectation of gross and the Holy Spirit and the deliverance from sin and aim that ministry to go forward and to be amazed and God's people to be free from guilt and the content to strike the enemy and knock him down and prefer to that and all the word you have use it and to live on the that and live on the impact and to unfold and to respond and to unite and to between the future of the impact of authority to be called on God and to be stronger and in 1st Samuel 13 says the windows of ministry the spear and use of it and the most of it your ministry and will go stronger and stronger to the Lord.

To feed the environment to be fed of the Spirit to have a vieu for the body of Christ and to connect the value to know the truth and to practice what you preach and to believe in a message and the idea of great trust and never have a short notice of a missing link of that situation because its like a oil and never dig a well and to be one accord and a generation and some place of time will be introduce in a rival in a strange thing in your life and to be set free in the Holy Spirit and the experience of the test of a favor and to be tracted and you have a relationship in Jesus and begin to move and to refirm and never missed the window of opportunity of a shield of protection to design to come in that matter and never be in a situation to be smash up because you will be and going to a level for a high calling in Ephesians Chapter 2 verse 1 and to receive the knowledge of Christ and the cooperation of a window of destiny and wisdom and revelation of the destiny and to the in spiritual growth in the Lord and to magnify the connection to grow in the future and to attend to preach the feeders and have a strong perfection and never have a combustion to our ministry and affect the enemy so he will not mess you up in that form.

These things we studied to plug in the future and the kingdom of God is the anointing of the spirit and make it click and the feeding by the word and to cast out demons and devour them and to commit in your ministry and to retain and great commission to be set free and the opportunities to get the people on track and the basis the discipline and to connect the missing piece of God's work

Darryl L. Mincey Man on a Mission Inc.

September 21, 1997

WORKING YOUR GIFT

Working and to know what you are and the gift of your lifework is more spiritual and the right opposition and specialized knowledge and to excel what ever to know what unique talents, abilities, spiritual gifts and anointing passions and great history and the expressions of Christ and use the ability to fly and the bible will say all things and the possitive thinking of faith and God will take the bad things out and the good things in life and have a purpose and to expect to preach and soar to the top and demonstrate the high calling in Ecc chapter 5 verse 18 (I have seen to be good) The market place and worship and prayer and all life is in Jesus and the ordinary thing to preach and God wants us to have the breakthrough and God will be your business partner.

In Genesis 15 in part of the language and able to master the situation of the progress and God will hear you and share your faith when you testify and in verse one of Genesis says fear not faith is the exportation of the positive note because the fear is a drag and that is a counterfeit image of the mistake of personal history even every day is a new day even repentance means to catch hold on 84% in your head is a great unconscious level and what can you do differently and a fresh revelation and to believe to account an performance and the provision and to grab hold to faith and believing the balance and there will be a breakthrough and when you have a situation there will be a breakthrough it will be a different one and now is the time to and the issue and to descend to your blood line and taking your ministry and to show you things to come.

In John chapter 15 verse one (The point of no return) and things in the spirit world and judge the world it is the cup of the man of nations and the cup of enity of mankind which Jesus did not drink it because it was the way of it and in 1st Timothy 5 verse 24, Genesis chapter 15 verse 17 The significance of covenant and God will call you to believe.

Darryl L. Mincey Man on a Mission Inc.

July 15, 1997

2ND KINGS CHAPTER 13
WHAT WE NEED TO DO IN A GOLD-HEARTED WAY:

And if we was not around we will be not around even in the street or some slum or buried and never get up from the ground were been written off, get down but never down in Jesus's land and have the power of influence and to changed one life and one word to one person and millions in time and one of things is having stock at word of life and invest and to get something that is the bow of ministry and the arrows that you have to identify the ministry and a small spear the boundaries but your garden will be small but the word of the lord will be there the garden of Eden was Adam's stopping ground and he made the mistakes and thats what he learn in the society and need to go in that situation and the salvation and a word in every church and every word into your life and the perfect time and sense the phrase of the word and this is that which is spoken and to meet you to prophet you and to develop the life you need and to read through the fellowship and the household of the church and which of that is spoken.

Certain times of the division of walking the right and comes in the spirit and seek the lord and all things will happen to take a bow of ministry and to practice the anointing and aim the substance of the direction of the word of churches and to be surrounded by the laying on the hands (1st Tim 1 verse 18) fight off this and have good fight and stand before God and drawn to him (still hold on and hold it) working that line of division and have a breakthrough to God and he will do the inside but we have the weapons of war and to direct the aim of it and give the enemy nothing because we are a cooperate church and the ministry will go higher and the gift will be there and it will give us a large occupation of ministry and and to aim and direct them.

A window of opportunity and the creation to create and develop a straight narrow margin to influence the training to be present and to perform to be open faithfully and give it the best shot you got and the Holy Spirit will be with you and the deliverance from sin and aim the point of sin to be removed and the ministry will go into high places and to be amazed for the good people and also to go places and the understanding by it and when you have the bow and arrow and to strike the enemy and to knock him down and kick his butt and to strike his release and to prefer to the word and use it all around and to live on the unfold and to respond to it and to unite and between the impact the opportunity and the truth and call on God and would have the now and to strike it hard and the only thing you will have this is in 1st Samuel 13 The windows of ministry the spear and the use of it and the most of your ministry will go stronger and stronger.

And all things in common to the inner man to a kingdom of environment and a culture of release to a view to connect the body of Christ and find a missing piece to believe a message to a great trust and never have a short notice of a missing ingredient and a temple of the reason why the flow and it is not long it's short and it's like a generation and one accord for one situation and to introduce a rival in strange things in your life and to be set free and to experiment and the point is there and favor and tracted and you have a relationship in Jesus you are friends with him and begin to move and to reaffirm to never miss out and the shield of protection will come in your crashing down because you will be recycling and never be smash and going to a level for a person calling in Ephesians chapter 2 verse one says the recivement of knowledge of Christ and to cooperate of a window of destiny and to obey the high calling of wisdom of revelation of the cooperate destiny and have a connection to grow upon and to be a member in God's kingdom and in the book of Ephesians 4 verse 11 says the gifts he gave were some would be apostles, some prophets, evangelists, some pastors and teachers and to equip and to large the great ones and to confirm into a strong perfection and never have a combustion to our ministry and to affect the enemy so he will not mess with you and your ministry its like a core group and to commit to ministry and to plug in the environment and to explore and to stay alive what clicks with you to anoint the word of God and the magnification and to cast out demons and model in the spirit and commit in your ministry and even on a mission to your harvest and a great commission to be free to your great destiny and finally the life skill and people who need models in the Holy Spirit and to get people on track and the basis and connect the missing piece.

Darryl L. Mincey Man on a Mission Inc.

9-26-97

WORKING YOUR GIFT PART TWO

Working and to know what you are and the gift of your lifework is more spiritual and the right opposition and specialized knowledge and to excel what ever to know what unique talents, abilities, spiritual gifts and anointing passions and great history and the expressions of Christ and use the ability to fly and the bible will say all things and the positive thinking of faith and God will take the bad things out and the good things in life and have a purpose and to expect to preach and soar to the top and demonstrate the high calling in Ecc chapter 5 verse 18 (I have seen to be good) The market place and worship and prayer and all life is in Jesus and the ordinary thing to preach and God wants us to have the breakthrough and God will be your business partner.

In Genesis 15 in part of the language and able to master the situation of the progress and God will hear you and share your faith when you testify and in verse one of Genesis says fear not faith is the exportation of the positive note because the fear is a drag and that is a counterfeit image of the mistake of personal history even every day is a new day even repentance means to catch hold on 84% in your head is a great unconscious level and what can you do differently and a fresh revelation and to believe to account an performance and the provision and to grab hold to faith and believing the balance and there will be a breakthrough and when you have a situation there will be a breakthrough it will be a different one and now is the time to and the issue and to descend to your blood line and taking your ministry and to show you things to come.

In John chapter 15 verse one (The point of no return) and things in the spirit world and judge the world it is the cup of the man of nations and the cup of enity of mankind which Jesus did not drink it because it was the way of it and in 1st Timothy 5 verse 24, Genesis chapter 15 verse 17 The significance of covenant and God will call you to believe.

Darryl L. Mincey Man on a Mission Inc.

July 15, 1997

2ND KINGS CHAPTER 13
WHAT WE NEED TO DO IN A GOLD-HEARTED WAY:

And if we was not around we will be not around even in the street or some slum or buried and never get up from the ground were been written of, get down but never down in Jesus's land and have the power of influence and to changed one life and one word to one person and millions in time and one of things is having stock at word of life and invest and to get something that is the bow of ministry and the arrows that you have to identify the ministry and a small spear the boundaries but your garden will be small but the word of the lord will be there the garden of Eden was Adam's stopping ground and he made the mistakes and thats what he learn in the society and need to go in that situation and the salvation and a word in every church and every word into your life and the perfect time and sense the phrase of the word and this is that which is spoken and to meet you to prophet you and to develop the life you need and to read through the fellowship and the household of the church and which of that is spoken.

Certain times of the division of walking the right and comes in the spirit and seek the lord and all things will happen to take a bow of ministry and to practice the anointing and aim the substance of the direction of the word of churches and to be surrounded by the laying on the hands (1st Tim 1 verse 18) fight off this and have good fight and stand before God and drawn to him (still hold on and hold it) working that line of division and have a breakthrough to God and he will do the inside but we have the weapons of war and to direct the aim of it and give the enemy nothing because we are a cooperate church and the ministry will go higher and the gift will be there and it will give us a large occupation of ministry and to aim and direct them.

A window of opportunity and the creation to create and develop a straight narrow margin to influence the training to be present and to perform to be open faithfully and give it the best shot you got and the Holy Spirit will be with you and the deliverance from sin and aim the point of sin to be removed and the ministry will go into high places and to be amazed for the good people and also to go places and the understanding by it and when you have the bow and arrow and to strike the enemy and to knock him down and kick his butt and to strike his release and to prefer to the word and use it all around and to live on the unfold and to respond to it and to unite and between the impact the opportunity and the truth and call on God and would have the now and to strike it hard and the only thing you will have this is in 1st Samuel 13 The windows of ministry the spear and the use of it and the most of your ministry will go stronger and stronger.

And all things in common to the inner man to a kingdom of environment and a culture of release to a vieu to connect the body of Christ and find a missing piece to believe a message to a great trust and never have a short notice of a missing ingredient and a temple of the reason why the flow and it is not long it's short and it's like a generation and one accord for one situation and to introduce a rival in strange things in lour life and to be set free and to experiment and the point is there and favor and tracted and you have a relationship in Jesus you are friends with him and begin to move and to reaffirm to never miss out and the shield of protection will come in your crashing down because you will be recycling and never be smash and going to a level for a person calling in Ephesians chapter 2 verse one says the recivement of knowledge of Christ and to cooperate of a window of destiny and to obey the high calling of wisdom of revelation of the cooperate destiny and have a connection to grow upon and to be a member in God's kingdom and in the book of Ephesians 4 verse 11 says the gifts he gave were some would be aposiles, some prophets, evangelists, some pastors and teachers and to equip and to large the great ones and to confirm into a strong perfection and never have a combustion to our ministry and to affect the enemy so he will not mess with you and your ministry its like a core group and to commit to ministry and to plug in the environment and to explore and to stay alive what clicks with you to anoint the word of God and the magnification and to cast out demons and model in the spirit and commit in your ministry and even on a mission to your harvest and a great commission to be free to your great destiny and finally the life skill and people who need models in the Holy Spirit and to get people on track and the basis and connect the missing piece.

Darryl L. Mincey Man on a Mission Inc.

9-26-97

DON'T LOSE YOUR TRACK

In 2nd Corinthians chapter 9 verse 24 to the 25th verse

Do you know that in a race the runners all compete but only on receives the prize? Run in a way that you may win it and athletes exercise self-control in all things; they do receive a perishable wealth, but an imperishable one so I do not run aimlessly, nor do I box through beating the air but I punish my body and enslave, so that after proclaiming to others I myself should not be disqualified.

Winning a race requires purpose and discipline. Paul uses his illustration to explain that the Christian life takes work, self-denial, and grueling preparation. As Christians we are running our heavenly reward. The essential discipline of the stama. Don't merely observe from the grandstand don't just out to a jog a couple of laps train diligently because your spiritual progress depends on it.

THE PURPOSE:

Run your race to win and run straight to the goal.

Don't get discouraged and never give up

THE PLAN:

Deny yourself whatever is potentially harmful.

Discipline your body and plant the good seed and look forward.

THE PRIZE:

A heavenly reward that never disappears.

THE ESCAPE:

Paul escapes death to start a fire to get rid of the viper and never puffs up with this attack and never gets caught because you will never reveal it and the rebellion to operate and the best reaction is to the surface and God will deliver you from your ememies and you it will never bite and also to a delivering to governing to a Judge and to seperate with deception because you are in a wrong crowd and the difference of principalities and the power of the stronghold and to get rid of the stronghold inspired pattern of thinking in 2nd Corinthians chapter 10 verses 1 to 4 a progressive years of warfare by that war and be victorious (Principality is the territorial rule of an unseen evil prince it may be geographical or institutional territory of may it follow other lines of association in which the nature of the personality of a fallen spirit secures it expression of people under it's influence and the atmosphere and the spirit of God will melt the demons.) The word repentance means repudiating our agreement with the enemies pretension thoughts and false beliefs and to get rid of the lawless and there is a such a thing called spiritual dropout if people are not saved in the Christian world to the principal of successful speres internal victory precades and external victory and God wants you to get the hooks off of you right now and give you a breakthrough in the generations of the Holy Spirit and the values of the goal and the level cooperate a wide level and to the nations and have a breakthrough and to occupy and to place that faith to come in and have the wisdom of faith and to fight off the flesh and choose and there is 4 thoughts 85% of thoughts are 300 words a minute and 1 only I knew about me and also the part what you knew about me.

The only thing to our standard living is to behave and have the right attitude to build upon it.

Sins of the father. Discerned and Renounced

Emotional Patterns. Incidents & Inquiries and to be recognized and to be healed.

Distorted. Beliefs and Inner vows must be defined and to replace.

Oppression. Dejected and to displace.

We must learn the word and to survived the experienced the Holy Spirit and never have pressure in your life and God wants us to have a overcoming spirit and never have a self destructed mind.

The warriors of the Lord will use the step of rivial and to the gentle of it will use in that form.

People in the right way of mind need some things to take care of because the Christian people are mixed in the world and try to saved unsaved souls and to see in that way and to pray to those who need it furthermore the ungodly people need attention and to bring prayers to help them and they will have head of instruction and to realize Jesus did not like destruction and the hard time of violence and feel an easy way to make it easy and to start to listen and everyone will come to a place to have peace and sometimes it works and allow different feelings and praying hard and the anger and depression will be remove and focus the love for Jesus and to stop holding things inside.

And Christians fall also sometimes if we are in the flesh and the world and come to reveal a winning deal and to have self control of the spirit and the circumstances and never get upset and tearing up the life your in but the excellence is not there and give God the situation your in and picture this, the anger is in one hand and Jesus in the other hand the right hand of course and the anger is dissolved.

And hard times will be removed and Jesus wants love and received love not hate and hold all the feelings and give the authority to God because he is the C.E.O in heaven.

The glory to the world is through the world because the peace must be there and the strife of the mindstorm and affect of the presence to push through us and to see us in the same way and to cover our ways to the Lord and to cleanse his lips and have the heart of God and his power and in Psalms chapter 145 says God is filled with love and is spoken and blessed you in the name of the lord and to share the word with the Lord and to meditate with the deeds with wonderful great things and to create the glory of the kingdom and the generation of all eyes and the open the light of them and rescue them and filled with beliefs and to praise to the lord and create with new things and to promote and to teach modern ways and to walk in the ways of the Lord and don't give up stay up and choose the Lord our God to love you and give you life.

Holiness is the life and to express in life and through us to be holy and to be joy and to fill and to the abundant in the word of the Lord and develop and to boast your image and in God's choice and your mind will transform a divine nature in the sense the progress and choose the command of God and the experience to grow in the kingdom. And a gift of God is good and the word of God will accomplish a goal and to perform a positive note to understand the progress of the wall of blessing and the wall of victory and to develop the gift of blessing and faith is strength and the fruit and to be whole and to accomplish to hear the sound of the Lord.

Darryl L. Mincey Man on a Mission Inc.

10-4-97

Give to God the first part of your life and the first part of your love and to get a vision in your life and give God the first portion and God will give you the rest and to focus your Christian life.

IMAGINE:

We can imagine the power of healing and God will help us with a situation of his scalpel and take control in our lives and his care and think of other decision to our responsibility to make a decision to our responsibility and to use our need and the will to prepare to manage in our steps and to turn our will to make it happen and the Lord will turn my life around and make it peacefully and to recover our source and the leap of faith and to follow God's guidance and without faith were useless and denial.

But we will not be shut out and never be down in our condition and to practice our steps to make it clear to kick out a burden and to set free in our lives and to be in God's love and full citizens in his great kingdom and never lose that step of mind and taste the victory of God and trust in the lord and to believe in him. And we choose the right thing by knowing what we know about yourselves in Christ and we must trust in the Lord because we must trust him in his eyes and in his heart and facing things that we must be very accomplish by choosing the right relationship with Jesus and other Christians and by affecting the only choice in our lives. We can see in our lives to heal others and sometimes bringing on yourselves and you cannot run to God and failure does not go with the Lord and disobedience will turn in a turmoil and some storms will continue and mostly problems we accede but faith will come and meet your needs and have steps, another area is power and if we maintain this is a problem and one thing is fear and it is the enemy's word and put this in our mind and worry about this because he is a deceiver and a liar and makes you weak and to snare but God will block it and will be healed by the power of God the joy of the Lord is our strength and never lose it in your ministry. And the lack of faith will never be because God will give you strength to give us faith without the lacking of your knowledge and the attitude, the relationship of Jesus is very important to ourselves and circumstances of life one time you can be upset by one little things but we ask God to help us with those little things.

Jesus always provided what we need in our spirit and the word of God will be a good one a provision will be accepted the words I've had will open the windows of heaven and the anointing and also be victorious because the Lord will be with us with the holy spirit and the river will never run away and it will be a year of the fix in Luke chapter 4. The ability to move to the house of God and the same anointing to be restore and the medicine of healing and have control and the peace of mind and the world and being perfect and the only present way to someone else and God talks to in a way of love and kindness but a lot of people can't hear him because a lot of people talk a lot but cannot hear and emotions have memories, and have total restoration and something will know the word.

In the book of James chapter 1 verse 21 says when you have a slingshot you are targeting someone who needs praying and to be save and be in truth and a layer of restoration and never be filthy in your mind and let the anointing soak and sacred experience in a way in protected word in the Lord even certain issues to people and put the works of the flesh and knock it off and let's get real in the Holy Spirit and alert in the bible and will speak to you and never be self-destructed and never be empty and never be injudgement and to know what we found in our hearts and never be in a lacking form and the holy word we be on your side in your christianality and learn to punch the target and the voice of the Lord will be with you.

And the strength of unity is a slingshot in 1st Samuel chapter 8 and chapter 9 verse 14 and in verse 16 to 21 we need a feeling of the Lord and make sure the nourishment is there and never be hungry in the word and your new body will be restored and to get rid of that stuff. We know about the holy pleasant feeling to yourself not to have a bad feeling to damage a situation for being this way to have a revelation in your spirit realm and the condition of life with God and a living experience to his love and to heal the hurt of your damages when you were younger in your childhood days on earth even in adulthood and the emotions of your life even reflecting fear and we must have faith and a good relationship in Christ and never be burden and the forgiveness will be there and to learn to trust in God and to relate in others and self-esteem and always be God - centered never be self-centered. Even try to prove yourself and to focus in God not the enemy and the only way to stay in the kingdom is to get off the baggage right out of your system

THE TARGET OF SPIRITUAL DIRECTION:

We focus what we know about yourselves in a spiritual direction is to have a target to aim to hit and what we need in our heart in Christ and have a point to a term to do is thing we can accomplished in our spiritual realm the distance we shoot and pull that bow and arrow and aim it to perfection why because we must be free from anything to punch out of the baggage and find a target of spiritual direction and to get rid of the junk inside us before it is too late to be safe but it is never too late and we will have a victory in God's kingdom.

The inprint of restoring the church and to hold off the past and never be bound and have a quick vision to be right and to be obedient and the proverb to a word to work overtime never to be in trouble and to locate your spiritual root and have abundance and find the fulfillment with Jesus and have the right thing in the spirit and have a multiply and have a breakthrough during your prayers in your life and God is a cheerful giver and to provide to encounter a powerful insight because God will wrestle but he will give you the gift of balance and to try to understand to reveal it. The programming yourself and the character flow and be anointed. The other man is your spirit man and the calling to produce your needs of the blueprint and to tap on it. And lingush and to inspire to worship God to do it and love knowledge and one part of anointing and the basic thing to confirm yourself talk and when talking but not hear it.

The internal dialog how to wax on and to wax off and to check yourself not to wreck yourself because we are renewing the spirit of our mind and every thought captive in Christ. I challenge every thought to make it line up with the following God desires that I have truth inward and therefore I speak the truth in my heart always.

In Jesus's name through the power of the holy spirit.

———————————————————

1. I now accept myself very total and unconditionally.

Ephesians 3 verse 17.

———————————————————

2. And be rooted in love and God's love for us in position.

———————————————————

3. I am now free from all self-destructive things

Romans 8 verse 1.

Darryl L. Mincey Man on a Mission Inc. October 13, 1997

Give to God the first part of your life and the first part of your love and to get a vision in your life and give God the first portion and God will give you the rest and to focus your Christian life.

IMAGINE:

We can imagine the power of healing and God will help us with a situation of his scalpel and take control in our lives and his care and think of other decision to our responsibility to make a decision to our responsibility and to use our need and the will to prepare to manage in our steps and to turn our will to make it happen and the Lord will turn my life around and make it peacefully and to recover our source and the leap of faith and to follow God's guidance and without faith were useless and denial.

But we will not be shut out and never be down in our condition and to practice our steps to make it clear to kick out a burden and to set free in our lives and to be in God's love and full citizens in his great kingdom and never lose that step of mind and taste the victory of God and trust in the lord and to believe in him. And we choose the right thing by knowing what we know about yourselves in Christ and we must trust in the Lord because we must trust him in his eyes and in his heart and facing things that we must be very accomplish by choosing the right relationship with Jesus and other Christians and by affecting the only choice in our lives. We can see in our lives to heal others and sometimes bringing on yourselves and you cannot run to God and failure does not go with the Lord and disobedience will turn in a turmoil and some storms will continue and mostly problems we accede but faith will come and meet your needs and have steps, another area is power and if we maintain this is a problem and one thing is fear and it is the enemy's word and put this in our mind and worry about this because he is a deceiver and a liar and makes you weak and to snare but God will block it and will be healed by the power of God the joy of the Lord is our strength and never lose it in your ministry. And the lack of faith will never be because God will give you strength to give us faith without the lacking of your knowledge and the attitude, the relationship of Jesus is very important to ourselves and circumstances of life one time you can be upset by one little things but we ask God to help us with those little things.

Jesus always provided what we need in our spirit and the word of God will be a good one a provision will be accepted the words I've had will open the windows of heaven and the anointing and also be victorious because the Lord will be with us with the Holy Spirit and the river will never run away and it will be a year of the fix in Luke chapter 4. The ability to move to the house of God and the same anointing to be restore and the medicine of healing and have control and the peace of mind and the world and being perfect and the only present way to someone else and God talks to in a way of love and kindness but a lot of people can't hear him because a lot of people talk a lot but cannot hear and emotions have memories, and have total restoration and something will know the word.

In the book of James chapter 1 verse 21 says when you have a slingshot you are targeting someone who needs praying and to be save and be in truth and a layer of restoration and never be filthy in your mind and let the anointing soak and sacred experience in a way in protected word in the Lord even certain issues to people and put the works of the flesh and knock it off and lets get real in the holy spirit and alert in the bible and will speak to you and never be self-destructed and never be empty and never be injudgement and to know what we found in our hearts and never be in a lacking form and the holy word we be on your side in your christianality and learn to punch the target and the voice of the Lord will be with you.

And the strength of unity is a slingshot in 1st Samuel chapter 8 and chapter 9 verse 14 and in verse 16 to 21 we need a feeling of the Lord and make sure the nourishment is there and never be hungry in the word and your new body will be restored and to get rid of that stuff. We know about the holy pleasant feeling to yourself not to have a bad feeling to damage a situation for being this way to have a revelation in your spirit realm and the condition of life with God and a living experience to his love and to heal the hurt of your damages when you were younger in your childhood days on earth even in adulthood and the emotions of your life even reflecting fear and we must have faith and a good relationship in Christ and never be burden and the forgiveness will be there and to learn to trust in God and to relate in others and self-esteem and always be God - centered never be self-centered. Even try to prove yourself and to focus in God not the enemy and the only way to stay in the kingdom is to get off the baggage right out of your system

THE TARGET OF SPIRITUAL DIRECTION:

We focus what we know about yourselves in a spiritual direction is to have a target to aim to hit and what we need in our heart in Christ and have a point to a term to do is thing we can accomplished in our spiritual realm the distance we shoot and pull that bow and arrow and aim it to perfection why because we must be free from anything to punch out of the baggage and find a target of spiritual direction and to get rid of the junk inside us before it is too late to be safe but it is never too late and we will have a victory in God's kingdom.

The inprint of restoring the church and to hold off the past and never be bound and have a quick vision to be right and to be obedient and the proverb to a word to work overtime never to be in trouble and to locate your spiritual root and have abundance and find the fulfillment with Jesus and have the right thing in the spirit and have a multiply and have a breakthrough during your prayers in your life and God is a cheerful giver and to provide to encounter a powerful insight because God will wrestle but he will give you the gift of balance and to try to understand to reveal it. The programming yourself and the character flow and be anointed. The other man is your spirit man and the calling to produce your needs of the blueprint and to tap on it. And lingush and to inspire to worship God to do it and love knowledge and one part of anointing and the basic thing to confirm yourself talk and when talking but not hear it.

The internal dialog how to wax on and to wax off and to check yourself not to wreck yourself because we are renewing the spirit of our mind and every thought captive in Christ. I challenge every thought to make it line up with the following God desires that I have truth inward and therefore I speak the truth in my heart always.

In Jesus's name through the power of the holy spirit.

---

1. I now accept myself very total and unconditionally.

Ephesians 3 verse 17.

---

2. And be rooted in love and God's love for us in position.

---

3. I am now free from all self-destructive things

Romans 8 verse 1.

Darryl L. Mincey Man on a Mission Inc. October 13, 1997

HONEST OF THE CHARIOTS

The east gate is the presence of the lord the sun will brighten up and God will rise up in the presence and he will be in control and continue and a place for it and have a question of Gods place or a gate and will open up a destiny of anointed purpose of the east gate and the appointed place and to be straight and tied all the total acceptance in Gods eyes and have a great moment and a great attitude.

God provide the vision of treasures when Jesus was born by raising. (Matt 2 verse 10) and in (1st Chronicles Chapter 29).

The temple of the Lord and the body of Christ and stretching the flesh and bring out the breakthrough and furthermore the Lord has a purpose what is given of gold and silver and the demonstration of the place of unity of freedom and the reflection of the house of God. We are known to be a Christian church and to have a spiritual fulfillment and have a function to know your calling because of the work of the church and open the door. In Luke chapter one verse 30 death is a cheating thing and living is a victory thing and your wound is a destiny and the ability to attend to a level what is the next step to divine a Christian knowledge and to become a part of the holy spirit and the same nature when you are real and a new creation and to reform the new birth and the next of kin and need to be close to God even when you are born again and to bring forth a perfect church and the birth of living and the creation of the holy spirit.

The honest thing to have is an hunger for God and the nature by it because we must be hungry for God and to be glorified and to seek him and the season of growth and the divine spiritual pattern and the sound of the earth and the sound of love and the great fruit of the season and sudden releases of God in Genesis chapter 1 says the divine word of God and feel the power and we must hear Gods commitment and when the spirit of love is around us the disaster must stop and to bring forth a healing insight of knowledge and the position of the light and it will shine upon us and when he reveals your name it will come out with authority and the old junk will come out the spirit of the light will never go out and it will be lit forever and the single day the touch of the spirit will be on the next level and light the candle.

The part of growing is very important and to discover the ways to know ourselves and the key of spiritual growth is important because it is never denial and that is the truth and to verify a pattern to solve a situation without fear and to repair the chariots we ride to and to concentrate our lives and to be healthy and we come a long way to strive of this and we must be equip and never be wounded and to increase signs and wonders and to bring up the harvest and let it grow and shine up the great heaven around us and the internal adjustment.

God created the heaven and the earth and it is a beautiful thing in divine and the earth was a steaming mess but God clean it up and the darkness had to be lifted up because we must believe in him and we did and they must know about a situation that will never fall because the enemy will use you in that form and give you false reasons but the light of God will give you freedom and you will be happy and to touch base and wipe out the bad form and nothing will hurt us in that form and we must trust God all the time and to anointed by the spirit and to be bless in the word and to stay strong riding those chariots and be the light of life and that period will perform.

Proverbs 15 verse 1 Search me o Lord and have something in my thoughts and know your hearts.

Darryl L. Mincey Man on a Mission Inc. October 15, 1997

54

THE HUMAN PART OF THE SPIRIT

Be fullness of love to be full of the great anointing and to be good to the lord and be bless and never leave your obedience of God because you will turn to be self-centered but the human part of the spirit wants to be God centered and base upon Christianity never tear it up because the enemy wants to tear you down but the lord will use his anointed power of love not to be fear and to rise you up.

But the enemy wants to curse you but Jesus will never leave the kingdom of God and the protection will be there because we must check it with the lord and to be risen and the anger will be removed and the curse will be broken and the wound will be healed and Jesus will healed others and the world and what he did and have a direction to be save by grace and the stream of God will be there and to be in control and praise the lord and the fine of faith is what given and the goods to enter the kingdom and the anointing of greatness will be in trans form the piece of re-shaping the changing of America and the holy spirit and the vessel of glory so we can use this situation and the root of amazing things to understand to conceal the image and to follow the work of God and to move the portion and to enforce the reshaping of it to know to fix because Jesus is the perfect one to minister and never be trapped by it sensors the opportunity that never borrowed and for the moment to be blessed and to change the city and the upper church and the kingdom of God and to filled the heart of soul and to begin to level to set the temple and to pour out the windows of heaven and the core of love and the life in the spirit and the house of God and the term the willing of pride the force.

And there is no fear in love and its faults and God will help your faults and never be trapped and have the faith in Christ and have a open heaven and it will never close it and the balance will be there and to prepare what to need to get rid of that form and get into the new and to reform to be God centered people and the holy spirit and never be self-centered because it is weak and the interesting time and say before that we know what to share in the word and to get in the spirit and the nation and to increase to create and to established new things and to grow and the unskilled the word of the right truth and to spend time in the lord and God will deliver us from bad times and never be in that division and to press on the direction of the foundation and to set free in the spirit and to develop great things to have a purpose and the doctor of love and to rise in the way to tell what God has allow the wisdom to need what we know and to walk with the spirit and to get rid of the baggage and never confuse correction and the light of light will be on our side and the vision to level it.

And it is the time to think what we know about the lessons to confirmed the value in power and to have timing is more important and the faithful in your ministry and to others and to flow in that point of willing and the great things to know the new level of the new birth and the adoption of Romans 8 verse 14 the anointing of the father and never suffer and get into the next level and the fellowship of faith and the things of the holy spirit and to learn how to walk in form and to rebuild and measure the things that we do for God and to maintain the revelation knowledge to perform the skill the style and the target the factor in the word of love and to flow to manifest and the high calling to determine the plan of the purpose and the members to exceed to us more and have the love what we need in the holy spirit and to multiply and the growth of it.

And the teaching of spiritual growth will be included by the information and the balance to use the vision of the city we live in and the word of God and also his kingdom and to influence the world and the attitude by the word and how do we emerge the living ways to contend to wash the old self into the new self and have a new life in the lord and to cut the bondage and to heal us to perfection and to be clean like Jesus that is why he went to the water and set people saved from the sins they made and also to repent and the power of freedom will be there and the light of life will be there in the spirit and to walk in joy.

Darryl L. Mincey Man on a Mission Inc. October 25, 1997

INCREASE THE FRUITFULNESS

We are moving on and the excellence to measure growth in God and in Galatians 5 verse 22 God made you a quickening of the spirit if you are faithful and faithful and give you provision and the fruit of the spirit is love, kindness and self control and the flesh is the passion of the spirit in the spirit and one of the way is called gifting and the ways for calling Isaiah 55 verse 8 the fruit of faithfulness will grow and to grow with a result and to grow in a situation and to nurture to each other and to be justified what we need to make a vow to be faithful established to grow of this matter and to glorified the lord and to lived on a high point and to choose the right thing and the brethren of the spirit will give you something in that anointing and never be stress to this situation and God will speak to you and in part of the message is God in my life and the progress of the fruit of the spirit realm and the fruit of faith James 2 verse 14 teaching how to trust the lord and you need a problem to have faith and give you a chance what God wants you to do and knew to trust God and to feel strong in faith and in prayer and to know what you feel better in your life and the door will be open for Jesus to come in and a blessing and make a difference and all the part of giving and the first fruit and the 200 people to bless the lord.

Encourage to go and to fasten upon to cure to help the ways and hear the voice of the lord and to build a courage to hold on and to live out the truth and to minister others and to fill the high calling and to express to bring life and in Hebrews 10 verse 19 to enter the blood of Jesus and watch what we say and the statement of harmony and to live the position and loving faith that works and born to be encourage and have strength and divine nature of relationships in Christ and also the church because it is made of people and about a tavern in Proverbs 18 verse

21 and in Proverbs 25 verse 23 The gift of gifting and the power of life and the power of the word and insight and to open the progress and to impact to layer our understanding to do well in the spirit of God and to be bless and the power of the holy spirit of knowledge is to be successful in your victory and there is a plan to tell you what you know and to explore the level of God and to manifest the body and to read the bible and to break depression and to have joy and in Psalms 110 you will have an increase and stop thinking small and have faith and have a great blessing with no sorrow with it.

The increase and affected by favor and more favor has a special advantage for success for a new level and committed in the importance of the right thinking to get a better level of the progress of the anointed of the overflowing cup and the blessing of god and to get more of him and to plant a source of completing the ways to follow the life you lived and all the words you are spoken to and God is a great God and put in the words in your program and the holy ghost will never fail and in Proverbs 6 verse 2 is to start talking to God and serve him and to seek God and his presence and to have faith and in 2nd Chronicles 26 verse 25 God made you prosper and God made you happen and the anointing of the ways to be ahead in Gods kingdom and let the cup overflow and the present of God will take care of business and the blessing of the holy ghost and to believe in the lord and to be prosper and to expect the following and to send a seed and what you reap and have faith and the harvest that is planted.

Darryl L. Mincey Man on a Mission Inc. October 31, 1997

THE VOICE.

The mount of Jesus Christ is in the anointing in me and the temple and the wonderful guidance and we do not to live in the dark the word of God is there on one to one basis in John 10 verse 27 to hear the voice of God and will give you a blessing with your finance and your families and you can set a place and you wont get ripped in personal things but God will help you in a personal guidance and hearing your voice and to have more time to fellowship with other Christians and never get switch off and God and the holy spirit will be your closest friend and when you have a anointing of the holy spirit and to be cleanse and the word of God will be there and the teaching of the voice is critical and important and a well meaning friend in the holy ghost and when God speaks to you it is there and a listening ear and a listening heart and you must stay in the holy ghost and god has a blue print for you and a divine gifting and a great direction and a spiritual guidance of this situation and be on the right hand.

THE RIGHT GUIDANCE:

The right guidance and the right faith and the right feeling and divine atmosphere Exodus chapter 24 verse 15 the cloud covered the mountains and angels are real the sign of God will defend us and to watch us and the love of an angel of the lord will be beside you and in the clouds and in the things to come and divine connection between connection and the offering and to supply the seed and to multiply and the harvest will grow and it will increase your financial giving and will bless and the heart of treasure the heart of Gods kingdom

Darryl L. Mincey Man on a Mission Inc. November 19, 1997

GETTING FED AND GETTING WELL

What we know about ourselves to move over the subject and need what kind of preaching we do for the Lord and no matter how you do we can do it right and to establish the needs of preaching and the words and to rise up others in those conditions. And have a moving part of a motivication in the Holy Ghost and called for the information and called the prompt of things. Religion is something and retain by biblical truth and God hears some people and not all people but God says all and removes all of it.

Revelation and motivation not the same well the exact way to do in that form and we do not enter a dead church we enter a alive church and kick the enemy's butt and be happy and to enjoy in the Holy Ghost and to stay in the right place and to never be on the wrong side. To follow the steps when you work we must be right on because God is watching us and the great issue of value of truth and to be free (I do not like religion) I believe in the spirit and a great vision of freedom and the stage of life and to be blessed Pray and to find what we know to be fed and to be strong to the high calling.

The first one is to be fulfill the harvest and to believe in Jesus and the generation of the earth. The bible says in Matthew chapter 23, A whole sermon is preaching and Jesus roasted the butt of religion and vow of lives and bring a new breed of understanding and God will heal you and to produce spirit life and the sound of generation and the balance of truth. To preach the word and the true thoughts of freedom and the depths of your spirit and to direct to rise up and never go down and a new brees will be born. The message of a mind set and to see God what we see todat and to show the ways to follow and how God is the teacher the everyday life and to touch the mind to others and to come across the community to discover the news of the lord and have much more and to received great levels opportunity and to grow in the field of harvest and where the treasure is to touch the heart and the issue and to be release what it is. In Proverbs 10 verse 5 says to cast down the water and to plant the foundation to established what we need for today and tomorrow. To increase the high level of anointing and to set forth and much more to open a view and value the treasure and the stuff what comes next. The instruction and a pattern is good but one thing to another is to sign, seal, and to deliver the importance of the harvest. The movement of the Holy Ghost and the greatness of God and to pray for the people and to live in Christ to fellowship and to hear the voice of the Lord and the greatness and to preach it and to serve an generation and to have a resource to follow the faith and never withhold.

Darryl L. Mincey Man on a Mission Inc. 12-8-97

THE STUFF THAT GOD DOES

Before the Army of the Lord and all the warriors before the Lord were too dangerous and they talked of strategy and the prevalence of sin and live in a whole group of this to be in form. And try to understand what is happening and focus your mind of the dealing to have an inheritance and to qualify the generation of high calling because the enemy will use the wrong doing in your life and God will give you the right and the things and the type of revelations. Joshua Chapter 5 says that the additions in water baptism will wash out the old self and fight off the flesh and the enemy and cross over the freedom land without the snake and to fight principalities because the flesh will mess you up because it is like a shadow and when God will use your circumcision of God will help you to stay like concerning fire and the flesh will not come near you. The response of this when God shows up the enemy will be mess up and be removed in the book of Joshua chapter 8 verse 5 says the circumcision will work and will be healed. To know what it is to have a flow of destiny and to remove the bitterness and the fiery darts will bounce off and never hit you because we are very strong in the Lord. The right thing is the right basic move to have and not to have a bondage to specify one to another but we are born again. God and his son defeated the problem and the failure and to knock off the old and put in the new of a real faith in your life. The Christ power will remove your guilt and take the possession of the death flesh into a born again

Christian because Jesus went to the cross and died for us. The healing of Christian is very important to us and to be blessed and to believe the power of the Lord and your rema and don't give the enemy any doubt because Jesus is anointed to have.

Darryl L. Mincey Man on a Mission Inc. December 15, 1997

THE UNITY OF UNDERSTANDING

Unity is very important to us and it is very important of Jesus because it will never have a government attitude and up to a point of view. The positive attitude is important the negative attitude must be removed and the curse of the warzone will be vomit. We must walk in unity never lose unity and the walking of God and the authority to be in the right hand of God and to be faithful to others in the Lord.

According to this topic is to listen God walks with patience and in Joshua Chapter 6, Crossover the freedom walk and God will give you the big vision and to manifest and to produce the privilege and to seek out the salvation and to reach out and the freedom will be there and hear Gods voice and present the ways to know not to compare from your destiny and stop looking at your past and let it go and to stay forward and the great ways to live and to attend to be a great provider and to measure the unity and to plant the seed and the walls of anger will come down and have a breakthrough and set a breakthrough and the victory will be there.

In Matthew chapter 13 The field is like a treasure and like a open heaven and healed up your wounds. God will give you a carnal visit and the lord will give you a realm to a reason to your circumstances and to worship you in the major league of the Holy Spirit and to have more in the bread of life. And give you life and somewhere in the future of the destiny to remove the problem and a situation for the release of my father's house and discover the light and feel great about it and a great gift of God.

When he sends them to the house and the desire with the form of measurement of God raise the generation and raising Davids and to be victorious to make a decision and to believe the to be wise and to the word of miracles and take what you have and the relationship and the anointing to one man. And the point of angels will help us to determine and to focus of the spirit and to hear his voice and the breakthrough will be there and to fill your life in the kingdom of God.

Darryl L. Mincey Man on a Mission Inc. December 15, 1997

THE FREEDOM BOAT

The purpose of this is the boat will never sink and it will tour all over the world even every country and in every city and every country of prayer and righteous things. And one thing that God wants us to rise up to take a challenge to knock off the darkness and open the light of life and the boat will not sink and to press the figure what we escaped from darkness because we cannot see but a candle will light it up and in John chapter 10 verse 10, The values of freedom and to attend to be victorious and the relations of Jesus to see the big life and the experience of the depth of the Holy spirit and the Christian life. To see what the people to see what they know about the point of excellence and the flow in the United States will have to know Jesus and the passion and the vision by it.

Darryl L. Mincey Man on a Mission Inc. 12-27-97